SAFETY FIRST

Safety on Your Bicycle

Joanne Mattern
ABDO Publishing Company

visit us at
www.abdopub.com

Published by Abdo Publishing Company 4940 Viking Drive, Edina, Minnesota 55435.
Copyright © 1999 by Abdo Consulting Group, Inc. International copyrights reserved in all
countries. No part of this book may be reproduced in any form without written permission
from the publisher.

Printed in the United States.

Photo credits: Peter Arnold, Inc., Super Stock

Edited by Julie Berg
Contributing editor Morgan Hughes
Graphics by Linda O'Leary

Library of Congress Cataloging-in-Publication Data

Mattern, Joanne, 1963-
         Safety on your bicycle / Joanne Mattern.
         p. cm. -- (Safety first)
         Includes index.
         Summary: Offers tips to keep young riders as safe as possible when riding a bike.
         ISBN 1-57765-073-5
         1. Cycling--Safety measures--Juvenile literature. [1. Bicycles and bicycling--
         Safety measures. 2. Safety.] I. Title. II. Series.
         GV1055.M38 1999
         796.6 028 9--DC21   98-17277
                                                                               CIP
                                                                               AC

Contents

Safety First!

Do you spend a lot of time riding your bike? Bicycles are a great way to get around. They are fast and fun! Riding a bike is great exercise, but it can also be **dangerous**. You'll have a lot more fun if you practice staying safe on your bike.

Staying safe means you won't get hurt. You won't get in trouble. And you will keep other people from getting hurt or in trouble, too!

How can you stay safe on your bicycle? The best way is to follow the rules and think before you act. This book will show you many ways to always put safety first while you are riding.

Opposite page:
Safe biking means
learning the rules.

Checking Your Bicycle

A bike has many different parts. All these parts have to work right for you to have a safe ride. Before you ride your bike, look it over. Make sure the tires have enough air in them. Check that the brakes work and that the chain is tight. Make sure the gears are working correctly and that the seat is the right height for you.

Parts of a bicycle that need to be checked.

If your bicycle has been in an **accident**, check it carefully before you ride it again. Make sure the frame is straight and that nothing is rubbing against the tires. If your bike is not working right, ask an adult to fix it before you ride it again.

If you haven't ridden your bike all winter, it probably needs a tune-up in the spring. Take it to a bicycle shop to be oiled and checked. Your bike will be as good as new!

Taking care of your bike makes it safer to ride.

Helmets

Every bike rider should wear a **helmet**. A helmet protects your head in case you fall off your bike or get in an **accident**.

Many states have laws that say all young bike riders must wear a helmet. Even if your state doesn't have this law, you should wear a helmet anyway. It could save your life. If you are wearing a helmet, you could walk away from a bad accident. That's better than ending up in the hospital!

Helmets aren't just for kids. If your parents or other adults ride bikes, ask them to wear one, too.

Opposite page:
Always wear a helmet
when riding.

Let People See You

If you ride your bike early in the morning or late in the evening, both you and your bike will be hard to see. The best way to stay safe is not to ride your bike when it is dark. If you have to ride at these times, there are some special things you can do to stay safe.

Make sure your bike has **reflectors**. These make your bike easier to see. Your bike should have at least six reflectors: one on the front, one on the back, one on each wheel, and one on the back of each pedal.

You can also make your clothes reflective. Some jackets have special reflectors on them. Or you can buy reflective tape and put it on your jacket or shirt. The brighter you are, the easier it will be to see you. And that's a great way to stay safe!

Make sure your bike has reflectors.

Rules of the Road

If you ride your bicycle in the street, you must follow the same rules that cars do. You should ride your bike along the side of the road in the same direction as traffic. You also have to obey all traffic **signals**, including red lights and stop signs. Never cut in front of a car or ride in the middle of a busy street.

Some people ride their bikes on the sidewalk or on marked bike paths. If you do this, be sure to look out for **pedestrians**. If your bike hits a person who is walking, both of you could get hurt!

Opposite page: Walk your bike across the street at a crosswalk.

When you cross the street, it's best to get off your
bike and walk it across. Make sure the light is
green. Use the crosswalk, and watch out for cars
turning in front of you. When you reach the other
side, lift your bike over the curb and climb back on.

Turn Signals

Cars have turn **signals** so drivers can let each other know which way they are moving. Bike riders should use turn signals, too. Turn signals are the best way to let drivers, other bike riders, and **pedestrians** know what you are going to do next. That means they can stay out of your way and you can stay safe.

To signal a right turn, hold your left arm out and bend it straight up at the elbow. Hold your hand up straight with the palm facing out. You can also signal a right turn by holding your right arm straight out.

To **signal** a left turn, hold your left arm straight
out. If you are going to stop or slow down, hold
your left arm so it is pointing toward the ground.

Right turn (optional right turn, left hand bent up at elbow)

Stop or slow down

Left turn

Stay Alert!

There are many things to watch when you are riding a bike. The most important thing to look out for is cars. The driver of a car cannot hear a bike. Sometimes he or she can't see it. It's up to you to watch for cars and stay out of their way.

Parked cars can be **dangerous**, too. If someone is getting out of a car and doesn't see you, he or she might open the door right into your path.

Bike riders also need to look out for **pedestrians**. If someone is walking in front of you on a sidewalk or bike path, call, "Excuse me" or "Watch out." You can also use a bell or a horn to tell people you're coming.

The best way to stay safe is always keep your eyes open and pay attention!

Watch for pedestrians when riding on the sidewalk.

Biking Etiquette

All bike riders should follow biking **etiquette**. Etiquette is the rules of polite behavior. Being polite is not only a good thing to do, it's a great way to stay safe, too!

Because bikes have to share the road with cars, etiquette is very important. If you're riding with a group of other bikes, ride **single file** so you can stay out of a car's way.

Another etiquette rule is not to weave in front of cars. This is true whether you are riding alone or with a group. And never do tricks on your bike. That includes "wheelies," riding with no hands, riding with your feet up, or letting someone ride on your handlebars.

It's best to ride single file.

Riding Off-Road

Some people like to ride their bikes **off-road**. They usually ride special bikes called **mountain bikes**. Mountain bikes are made to take rough conditions. They have heavy tires and other features that help them ride over bumpy ground.

If you ride your bike off-road, make sure it can take the rough conditions. Mountain bikers also wear special gear to protect themselves. Along with a **helmet**, you should wear padded gloves to protect your hands. Some bikers also wear pads on their knees and elbows to protect them in case they fall.

It's a good idea to learn about off-road biking before you try it. Join a local club or talk to other bikers about the best and safest ways to ride off-road. Your library may have books on the subject, too. The more you know, the more you can put safety first!

A mountain bike is built for off-road riding.

Glossary

Accident (AK-si-duhnt) - something that takes place without planning it.

Dangerous (DAYN-jur-uhss) - likely to cause harm; not safe.

Etiquette (ET-uh-ket) - rules of polite and proper behavior.

Helmet (HEL-mit) - a hard hat that protects your head during sports or dangerous activities.

Mountain bike (MOUN-tuhn bike) - a strong bicycle with many gears and heavy tires that can be ridden on rough or hilly ground.

Off-road (AWF rohd) - operating away from public roads.

Pedestrian (puh-DESS-tree-uhn) - someone who travels on foot.

Reflector (ri-FLEK-tor) - a shiny surface that bounces back light.

Signal (SIG-nuhl) - a sound, motion, or object that sends a message or warning.

Single file (SING-guhl FILE) - one after the other, in a line.

Internet Sites

Bicycling Safety
http://www.cam.org/~skippy/sites/cycling/SafetyLinks.html
Stories, studies, statistics, and tips on everything from safe cycling practices to maintenance. Special interest sections for kids and parents, and links to many interesting sites!

Safety Tips for Kids on the Internet
http://www.fbi.gov/kids/internet/internet.htm
The FBI has set up a "safety tips for the internet" website. It has very good information about how to protect yourself online.

National School Safety Center
http://www.nssc1.org/
This site provides training and resources for preventing school crime and violence.

Home Safety
http://www.safewithin.com/homesafe/
This site helps to make the home more secure, info on the health of the home environment and other safety resources.
These sites are subject to change.

Pass It On

Educate readers around the country by passing on information you've learned about staying safe. Share your little-known facts and interesting stories. Tell others about bike riding, school experiences, and any other stuff you'd like to discuss. We want to hear from you!

To get posted on the ABDO Publishing Company website E-mail us at **"adventure@abdopub.com"**
Download a free screen saver at www.abdopub.com

Index